The Mystification of Elle Pelham: Random Thoughts

AF471899

The hysterical nature of depression creates the most beautiful prose-urgent, emotional and truthfully cathartic.

Flora.

like a rose that has yet to bloom
after the first cut
during winter pruning
my heart was waiting
for
him
and his green thumb
He knows how to take care of me
how to nurture me through every cycle
he knows how to make me
bloom
Despite the frost that slows down growth
I grew
He put in work and all the extra attention I needed
He fertilized me and
thumb pruned my rose brush,
leaving me with only the very best stems...
A single bloom or a spray?
Either way he still thinks I'm beautiful
so careful while he debudded me
no scars on his exhibition rose
I
bloom
In his eyes his rose is a masterpiece
In his eyes I'm
perfect.

Stupefied.

POISON.

I wanted you to open up to me
I wanted you to open me up
but sometimes love and lust make a dangerous cocktail
I'd rather you pour your heart in my cup
than use your piece as my straw
So pour me a shot, babe
pour me a glass of your trouble
My hangover'll be like a high on some 70s psychedelic type shh
happy
carefree
just higher than a mofo for no doggone reason at all
When you seep through my pores I'll sweat you out
but I'll still have your scent on my dress
My breath will smell just like you and
those who don't understand will be like "Your breath reeks. You're
stupid drunk"
So the next time I see you kiss me
I want to see if it feels like liquor hitting my lips or
water washing over me…

Noise.

An electric guitar plays in the background
as i go over sheet music that means absolutely
nothing
i stare into space and dream about
my own hands
strumming the strings of that guitar
no rules
just ruthless
no pick
no treble clef, no time signature, no sharps or flats
just me
strumming the strings of that guitar
like i don't have no got-doggone sense
sing to me baby
i'll push my music stand to the floor and watch each sheet fall
and watch me fall
deeper
as you hummm to me
i'm falling
as i hold that guitar close to me
nobody's here to see us
i got you baby
let me pluck those strings as hard as i can
and i'll sing with you
let's sing as loud as we can
yeah that's the right chord

i feel you baby
and then i feel you fall from my hands
the perfect dream is my favorite nightmare
get you, got you, gone
i pick up my music stand, put my sheet music back in order
and just when i get ready to play i see you again
this time i won't drop you
because you'll be
holding me
strumming me
hummm
yeah you can have me
i'll be your guitar and
you'll sing with me
never put me down because you'll never hear this song again
keep playing this guitar because you don't want this song to end
i got you baby
i feel you baby
no rules, just ruthless
just me
and....you.

Ethereal.

I met you in another lifetime
A long time ago when I was me
and you were really you
(think about fireflies and fireworks and well, fire....)
I saw your face for the first time and you
grabbed my hand
I got that Uneasy Feeling like
butterflies
flying around in my gut
and it blew my mind
How can one face suck me in
and grab me by the heart
so fast
One hand on my heart and one hand in mine
with such a tight grip
and then you let go and you disappeared
Now I can't see you
I hear your voice but I can't hear you
and I am listening
I'm reaching out to you and I don't feel your hand
but I still feel your hand on my heart.
You let go and now we go around and round in circles
flying down 285 and you're swerving in and out of traffic

(I guess this is what happens when I let you sit in the driver's seat)

I want to get out of here!

I don't like going loopty-loop

and I will tell you to slow down

I'll reach my hand out one more time and this time

don't let go

Maybe one day I'll wake up and be able to say

Good morning

it's nice to see you again....

Watch.

like clockwork...
Twelve o'clock midnight
is it twelve in the morning or is it late at night?
adjust your clock my friend
this is my time not yours
you're on my watch
I like to watch the sun rise but
I like to see the moon even more
dark
scary
and beautiful all at the same time
fast forward
twelve thirty
not quite a straight line
curved enough to be
crooked
A crook in the night can
still rob you in the day
Still
STILL.
What happens in the dark
will soon come to light
sunlight
twilight
moonlight
Twelve forty-five

adjust your clock my friend
this is my time not yours
you're on my watch
It's almost one
one and done
Lights Out.

Drive.

I'm low-riding in my Honda
speeding down the street
stop
red light
catches me
Sixty down to
zero
but my adrenaline is still pumping
what am I gonna do with all of this built up tension?!
GREEN LIGHT
Gone
green means it's ok to go
it's ok to keep going
but proceed with caution and don't speed
there's a yellow light coming up soon
stay at a steady speed
and never come to another red light
keep riding until I approach Destiny
when I arrive I'll know I'm in the right place
but I'll never find out unless I
keep riding…

Disintegrate.

I will come to you
I will bring you all of me
I will give you all of me
take me
have me
and let every piece of me
fall
into your arms
crumble
and melt away
Can you feel me even when I'm
too far gone?
Do you know I'm still there
even after I've left you?
Let's dance
and let me melt away
watch me melt away
After I crumble
and fall into your arms.
Oh what a mess you have on your hands
Will you wipe me up with a sponge
and absorb me?
Will you dip a napkin into my puddle
and wipe me clean?
Will you put a sign over me
CAUTION: WET FLOOR

and wait for the cleaning man to take care of me?
Or will you come, Mr. Maintenance Man, and come
take care of me?

Rapport.

I close my eyes and I see your face-
brown eyes opened wide, filled
with all kinds of emotions and
ready to cry
Let those tears fall so I can really see you
I want to feel you really close
even though I've never seen or felt anything like you before
There is something about those brown eyes that keeps me coming back
coming back wanting to know more
wanting to keep my eyes closed and see more of
you
I'm scared
that if I open my eyes you'll disappear
this vision of you that I've sketched with your tears will
evaporate
but maybe I need to open my eyes to see
through the mirage of what's not there
and to see what's been there all along...

Aviary.

I'm tired of mending broken birds
and then they fly away
No "thanks for the pick-me-up", no signs of gratitude
they just fly away
They always come in the same shape-
broken down, no sense of direction, nobody to love them
and then I come in and save the day
give em a reason to live and get out there and
fly again
I repair those wings and sometimes give em new ones
and more than knowing I love em they can
feel love
One stupid bird I fixed up from top to bottom
and guess what?
He stayed. But it wasn't for long
it wasn't forever
but even before I let em out of his cage
I already felt like he had flown away
So now I'm empty
no more energy to spend on making bird cages
or time to spend wrapping up broken wings
in fact, I have nothing left for me
So now I feel like forget them,
forget all of those birds out there flying around like they did it all alone
and even have the nerve to bring another bird to the nest I built
Oh no! No more mending broken birds for me

I think it's time to pursue a new career as a hunter
and right the wrongs of the crimes committed in the sky:
too many birds flying around and flying too high...

lady.

I am a woman
and I don't like red
Why?
Because it reminds me of
stop lights and stop signs and everything that yells
STOP
the color of a teacher's pen when she tells you you're wrong
(and we all know that X marks the spot)
lipstick that's too bright
neon lights in a dark
alley inviting you to come on down
the forbidden color nailpolish a little girl can't wear because it's a
"grown woman's color" and get stuck with bubblegum pink or clear
(BREATHE)
the color that's supposed to represent love and gets replaced from time
to time by pink because it's a softer color when we all know that love is
hard (BREATHE!)
it makes me feel angry-
maybe because it is everything I am supposed to be and
everything I'm not...

Perception.

The moment that fist struck the right side of my face
the shackles came off
a beast came out
somebody I never saw before and
apparently neithcr had he
I was.....what word fits in the blank?
Free?
unchained, untied, no ring on my finger anymore
yeah, that sounds about right but it's something deeper than that
Released?
unconfined, unrestricted, unrestrained
hmm, I think that's a little closer but
there's more
Definitely liberated
open-minded, free thinking, enlightened
My mind was free to think. Wow
so there were chains on my mind?
was it in a cage?
How did my mind get....stuck?
I don't know, but as soon as I felt five knuckles meet my jawline
I was set free
I was....
Delivered.
It was like looking in the mirror and seeing myself for the first time
Like I was a mother looking at her daughter and seeing herself
Wow

I got to see myself
for who I really am-
Not a victim
but a victor.

Hysteria.

The early hours of morning
are when these thoughts cross my mind
There are 187 square tiles on the floor
and so far I've counted 2,492,186 ridges in the ceiling
I see my handprint on the wall
next to three little scratches on my headboard
I can hear my heart racing against my chest, well,
my mind actually
seeing which one is going to give in first
I can't sleep because
it's four o'clock in the morning and
this is when those thoughts start creeping into my mind
playing again like a horror flick soundtrack
where the beautiful melody of the piano gets drowned out
by the haunting screams of some famous rocker and his stupid guitar
(I used to like the guitar once upon a time...)
and the drums play real loud to the point where it's
deafening
WHY CAN'T I GET YOU OUT OF MY HEAD!
Now I'm screaming with the rocker
FORGET YOU FOR IGNORING ME! I HATE YOU FOR TREATING ME
LIKE THIS!
but silence fills the air and no one can hear me
No one can hear me.
Dang, that's kinda messed up
you won't come save me

now there's four scratches on my headboard
and another handprint on my wall
Now another day is dawning on me
like I had a one-night-stand with the moon last night
sunrays slipping through my window slapping me
WAKE UP CHICK!
I was asleep?
This was a dream?
Walking around with my eyes wide shut.

Taken.

I want him
but he's unavailable
I call his heart
but I never get an answer
I fight to knock down walls of steel
and still
with bloody knuckles I get up and fight
against them
against him
against me
against me?
yes she
is my biggest enemy because
when the mind knows what it wants it wants
when the heart loves it loves
and that leaves me to keep calling a heart that never answers me
a man unavailable
me wondering if he'll ever take the Do Not Disturb sign out of the door
if he'll ever open it
will he ever let me in?
does he even care that i'm still standing there?
should i walk away with two middle fingers in the air
or should i break down the door and show him i care?
it's not fair
i'm the woman in this
he should be the one with the bloody knuckles

he should be the one fighting but
he's not

•

he's not.
my heart hits the floor
shatters
and he's unavailable
to pick up the pieces
but at least i can take his pants off
stomp away in my stilettos
and slam the door behind me...

Redemption.

You need to be saved from yourself
Who's gonna rescue you now?
You hide from me
not realizing that I can see you
I can really see you
An SOS answered but
a lifejacket ignored
I want to shake you
but perhaps you're already shook
You think you can get out of the water on your own when you've been
Drowning
Go ahead, Poseidon, do it your way
Fall to the
Bottom
I'll meet you there and swim up with you
I can't carry you because you're too heavy but
I'll swim with you
Follow me
Don't you trust me?
This is not the ocean it's a toilet bowl
You're swimming in your own ish
and silly me,
I'm swimming with you
So answer me, Boss Man,
who's gonna rescue you now?
Are you gonna make your Great Escape or

Are you gonna keep pretending you don’t see me?

Missing.

The world is flying past me and I'm standing still
I'm standing still
Despite all the ish going on around me
What in the world is going on by the way?
I scratch my head and realize I really don't know what the heck is going on.
I'm at an intersection and I don't know where I am
Not a got-dern clue
So many smiling faces
They make me so flipping angry
tears falling down and they keep
Passing me by
I'm just another face I suppose
Nothing special
Nothing good enough to make the world
Stop
No one understands
And they probably never will
Because they're too busy living their own lives
to give a dern about what's going on in mine.

Exposed.

Come watch me strip
Strip
Down
To absolutely
Nothing
Bare
Come see me
You should take a look at it
I know you want to know what's been
Hiding
Underneath
All these clothes
Don't you want to see me
All of it
From the roots of my hair
To my pinky toenail?
Well baby, you've got to get
Close
And go all the way
Down
To see me
Naked.

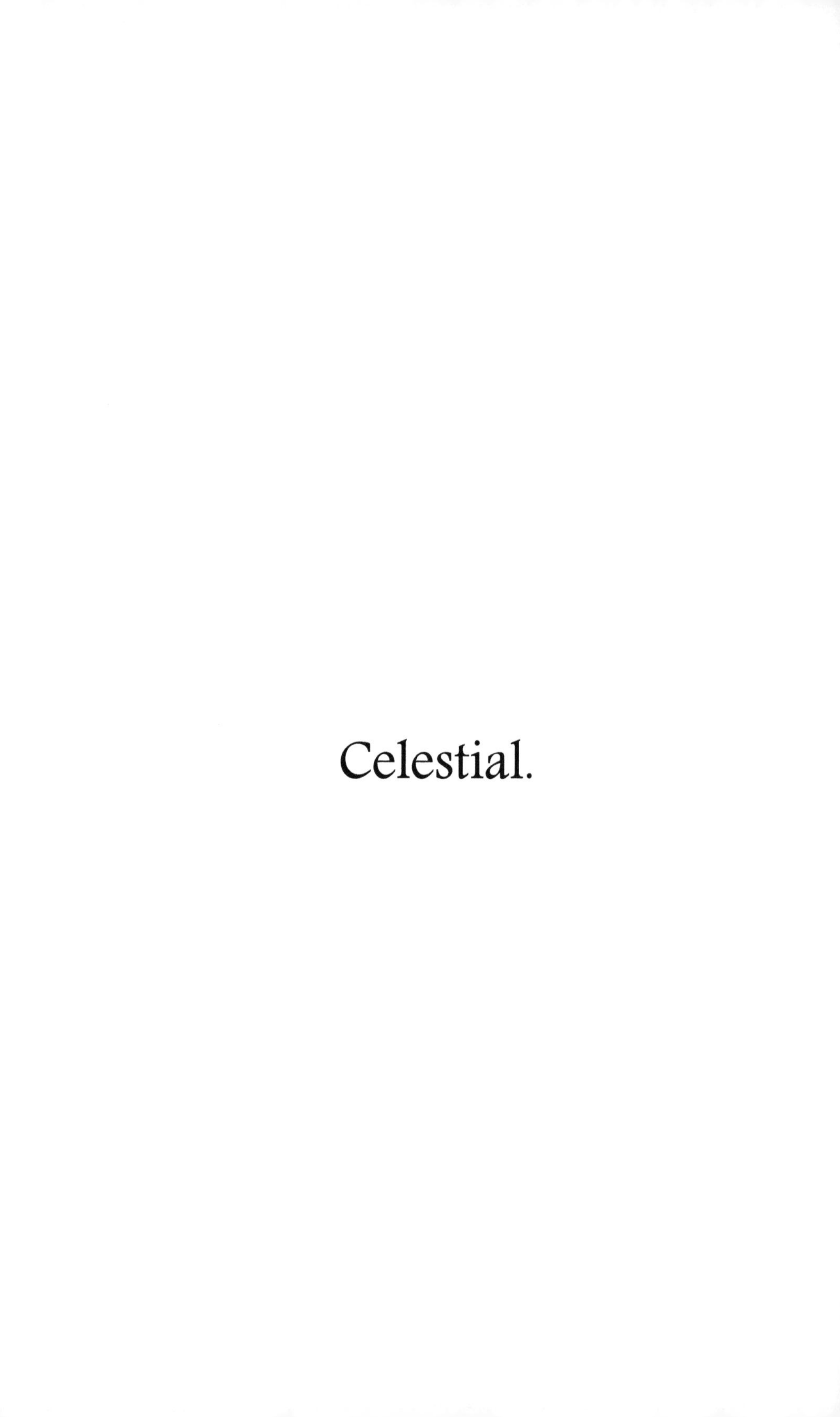
Celestial.

You fell back down to earth
it brought me close to you
Now is the time you're most inclined towards the star you orbit.
Now is the time to step into the longest period of daylight.
When the nights are short and the sun reaches
its highest position in the sky,
Recognize your star,
see what time it is,
and don't be afraid to orbit around the sun–
the light she'll shine down on your world
will give you life.
Summer Solstice.

Tempest.

As the saying goes, when it rains it pours
but no one say anything about a
hurricane
A thunderstorm is one thing
even a severe one
but it still doesn't compare to the effects of a
hurricane
A Watch was issued
and ignored
Experience with bad storms made me blind
to the fact that this was different
it wasn't the same thing I've faced before
So now it's raining
and a piece of hail
slapped me across the face
Eff you, weatherman
I'm not prepared for the hell
I'm about to face
My windows aren't boarded up
I don't have any batteries
or a flashlight or a radio
My gas tank is
empty
A Hurricane Warning is in effect
The wind blew my boards away
The line is too long at the store

I ran out of gas on the way back and now I'm
stuck
in this position until the hurricane passes over
and who knows what type of damage
I'll be facing
in the morning…

confusion.

I froze in my tracks
my mind entered the twilight zone
my heart dropped to the pit of my stomach
and I slapped myself silly
Aas soon as I saw you
How did we get here baby?
Where did we go wrong?
I'm miserable- are you?
Do you miss me? I miss you.
Why am I standing apart from you instead of finding
comfort in your arms?
And then I remember
The flashbacks of the good, the bad, and the ugly start
flooding my brain
And the love I feel for you starts
Flooding my heart
Two months of being without you and I don't know why
I'm sitting here in a suit and I don't know why
I want you so bad and I don't know why
I still want to love you.
I want to scream at the top of my lungs
I LOVE YOU CAN'T YOU SEE?!
but all I can do is look away
I can't face the idea of seeing you and not being with you
My heart still belongs to you and no matter how many times I change
the locks

you always find your way back in
I can't help but fall in love with you
over and over again
despite the heartache that results every time
Am I a fool for thinking this time will be different?
Am I foolish for thinking there will even be a next time?
My mind has had enough of the twilight zone and as I snap back to reality
I thaw out
and all that's left of me is
condensation…

viva.vida.

slip on your highest heels

hike up your tightest skirt

it's happy hour honey

I've been thinking about that Long Island Iced Tea

All day

It's time to play

So put on that lipgloss girl

Shake your hair out of that bun and make it look

Crazy

Let's shown 'em we're crazy

And they need you

Like I need that drink

Nah eff that

I don't need that

Or anything

Or anyone

But I'm about to go out and have fun

As soon as I get out of the mirror

Dang I look good...

Watch me go to work.

Spellbound.

he drives me crazy

sometimes it pisses me off

sometimes it turns me on

but it always makes me yearn for more

he's already a star in my eyes but

he wants to be accepted by the world

I'm already a part of his world but

somehow it's not enough and

it always makes me yearn for more.

He's mean, sweet, passionate, emotionally closed off sometimes

He kind of reminds me of a pimp sometimes

Is that why I'm drawn to him? (a pimp? *Really?*)

Haaa the crazy logic that formulates in my mind

Clicks

with the craziness that comes out of his mouth

and vice versa

He's so doggone sexy to me

for so many reasons

mostly because the key to his heart is intangible (but not unattainable)

and my appetite for him is insatiable.

When I ask him where his head is at my

inquiry is met with silence or

a response I'd have to decipher using hieroglyphics

But if he can picture it so can I

Once I figure him out I'll make that good grade

and we can be living that good good life.

Smashed.

After all of this

Perhaps I'm delusional.

....

The arrow that pierced my heart-

Pure gold, sharper than the strike of lighting-

Is permanently lodged in my chest.

Internally bleeding

Eternally weeping

I find something so delicious about this pain

I even told Elizabeth that this is The Big One.

I can taste it on my lips

After lyrical emesis

Caused by an overflow of the contents of my diaphragm (probably butterflies)

Or a regurgitation of one of my heart valves (damaged).

It's emotionally intoxicating

Pacifying me with a vision of passion and romance that is clearly an illusion. Isn't it?

What's going on?

In a moment of rare (in)sanity I look down at my chest and realize that I have been

Lovestruck

But in some sick way

the pain feels so good I feel

Lovestoned.

Puff, Puff. Passss.

When it's never good enough and you've gave it all you can and there's nothing left to do but cry or die you look at the choices you're given take a good long look over your life and decide if you need to leave well enough alone. Ha what a horrible saying that is I can't stand it especially when things aren't going well you want to tell me to leave well enough alone? That's foolishness it doesn't even make logical sense so what I do instead is say a big "eff you very much" to my troubles and the people causing them and let my pen hit the paper. I am not responsible for what happens next.

The.End?

www.ingramcontent.com/pod-product-compliance
Ingram Content Group UK Ltd.
Pitfield, Milton Keynes, MK11 3LW, UK
UKHW041840200726
13854UKWH00003BA/1236

9 781300 646402